ENGINEERING MARVELS OF AUSTRALIA

Australia's Railways

Alison Hideki

REDBACK publishing

Redback Publishing
PO Box 357
Frenchs Forest NSW 2086
Australia

www.redbackpublishing.com.au
orders@redbackpublishing.com.au

978-1-922322-12-8

Author: Alison Hideki
Editor: Michael Anderson
Proofing: Marianne Lindsell
Designer: Redback Publishing

Original illustrations © Redback Publishing 2020
Originated by Redback Publishing

Printed and bound in China

Acknowledgements
Abbreviations: l—left, r—right, b—bottom, t—top, c—centre, m—middle
We would like to thank the following for permission to reproduce photographs: (Images © shutterstock) p6b - The Great Zig Zag 1877, Nicholas John Caire, State Library VIC, p8b - Group of men working on the railway, 1890, State Library VIC, p9t - Tramway construction 1925, State Library VIC, p9b - Cameleers with Afghan drivers, 1930, State Library VIC, p16b - Trans-Australian railway by Bahnfrend via Wikimedia, p17t - Packing timber during construction of line, PIC/8736/14 LOC Box PIC/8736, National Library Australia, p8m - Laying the Trans-Australian Railway line, 1916, State Library of Western Australia, p21m - Parliament Station platform by Teknorat via Wikimedia, p21b - Caufield group City Loop portal by Marcus Wong via Wikimedia, p26m - QR Tilt train at Bowen Hills by Byrd250k via Wikimedia

Every effort has been made to contact copyright holders of any material reproduced in this book. Any omissions will be rectified in subsequent printings if notice is given to the publisher.

NATIONAL LIBRARY OF AUSTRALIA

A catalogue record for this book is available from the National Library of Australia

Contents

Transporting People and Goods 4
The Lithgow Zig-Zag Railway 6
The Central Australian Railway 8
- Upgrading the Line 10
- Extending the Line 12

The West Coast Wilderness Railway 14
The Trans-Australian Railway 16
- Construction in the Desert 18

Melbourne City Loop 20
- Constructing the Loop 22
- Loop Technology 24

Queensland Tilt Train 26
Railways at a Glance 27
Railways Snapshot 28
The Future of Rail in Australia 30
Glossary 31
Index 32

Transporting People and Goods

Australia's railways are marvels of engineering construction and technology. They provide transport in cities and suburbs, in some places underground, and away from the cities they cross the plains and deserts of the Australian continent from north to south and from east to west. They pass through hilly and mountainous areas, through deep cuttings, across bridges, and through tunnels blasted and drilled through solid rock. Everyday, they carry millions of people and they transport goods and raw materials to play an important role in the business activity of the nation.

STEEL ROADS

Railway tracks are steel roadways. Parallel steel rails are fixed to sleepers that run crossways beneath them at regular and close intervals, usually 0.5 metres. To prevent them from moving, the sleepers are set on a bed of crushed rock called ballast.

GUAGES

The distance between the parallel rails of the track is called the gauge. Gauges can vary from railway to railway. Narrow gauge lines are best suited to terrain that has many sharp bends and curves, but this limits the speed of the trains. Broader gauges allow for greater speed, but the tracks cannot have sharp bends. Narrow gauge lines are the cheapest to build. The world's most common gauge is 1.437 metre (4 feet 8.5 inches), commonly known as standard gauge. The wheels of the train run on the flat tops of the rails. A lip called a flange on the inside of the wheels prevents them from moving sideways off the rails.

Gauge Madness

Trains are built to fit a particular track gauge. Their bogeys (set of wheels) are set at a certain width apart to match the track they will travel on. In the early 1850's the colonies of New South Wales, South Australia and Victoria agreed to build railways to the 5 feet 3 inch gauge (1.6 metres). The New South Wales Government then changed its mind and built to the standard gauge, 4 feet 8.5 inches (1.437 metres). Victoria and South Australia had already ordered the rolling stock (trains and carriages) for the wider gauge. Queensland, Western Australia and Tasmania built the narrow 3 feet 6 inches (1.068 metres) gauge because it was cheaper. South Australia also built some of the cheaper narrow gauge railways. This meant that in many cases trains could not travel across the state borders. Passengers and goods had to be transferred to a different train whenever there was a change of gauge.

THE GRADIENT

Building railways involves more than the laying of tracks. Trains cannot climb steep hills. Their steel wheels running on steel rails give them much less traction than a car or truck has on a road surface. Tracks therefore have to be kept as level as possible. When a track does have to rise, the incline must be kept to a minimum. Inclines vary, but most are approximately one metre for every 100 metres of distance travelled. A rise of one metre in 75 metres is steep. This measurement is called the track gradient.

Technology Time Machine! Bogey Exchange

In 1952, a system of bogey exchange was developed in Victoria. It overcame the problem of having to transfer goods from one train to another when a line changed gauge, such as at Albury on the Melbourne to Sydney line. The freight wagons were lifted off their bogeys and placed on bogeys that could run on the line taking the freight to its destination. The system was used until gauges were made consistent in the late 1960's.

CUTTINGS, TUNNELS AND BRIDGES

To avoid steep inclines, massive earthworks often have to be carried out. Cuttings must be hacked through hills, or embankments must be built along hillsides to allow the track to rise gently along the side of the hill. Sometimes tunnels are blasted or bored through mountains when no alternative route is available. Bridges have to be built to carry tracks across ravines and rivers.

The Lithgow Zig-Zag Railway

Lithgow Zig-Zag line was built between 1866 and 1869 to carry farm produce across the Blue Mountains to Sydney, and to provide a service for the mining of coal and iron ore deposits in the Lithgow area.

AN ENGINEERING CHALLENGE

New South Wales railway engineer John Whitton was faced with the challenge of the steep descent from the mountaintop to the valley of the Nepean River below. The funds needed for a long tunnel (3.2 kilometres) through the mountains to keep the rail line on a fairly gentle slope were not available. Whitton solved the problem by building a line in the shape of a Z (a zig-zag). At each point of the Z, an extension line allowed trains to run off the Z, and then reverse to travel along the next leg of the Z. One of these extension lines ended at a vertical rock-face. Another ended at a wooden barrier at the edge of a vertical cliff. But even with the zig-zag design, the line gradient in some parts was extremely steep for a train – a rise of one metre in every 42 metres.

CONSTRUCTION

The path of the Zig-Zag track was carved into the cliff, and an embankment was built to hold it from slipping down the cliff. Three viaducts were built to carry the track across steep ravines. Two tunnels, one 450 metres long, were built. Dynamite was used to blast rock, but men used picks and sledgehammers to break it up, and shovels to load it onto horse drawn carts for removal. Men lugged sleepers, and teams of them hauled lengths of steel rail into position on the sleepers. What machinery there was - scoops and graders - was hauled by draught horses.

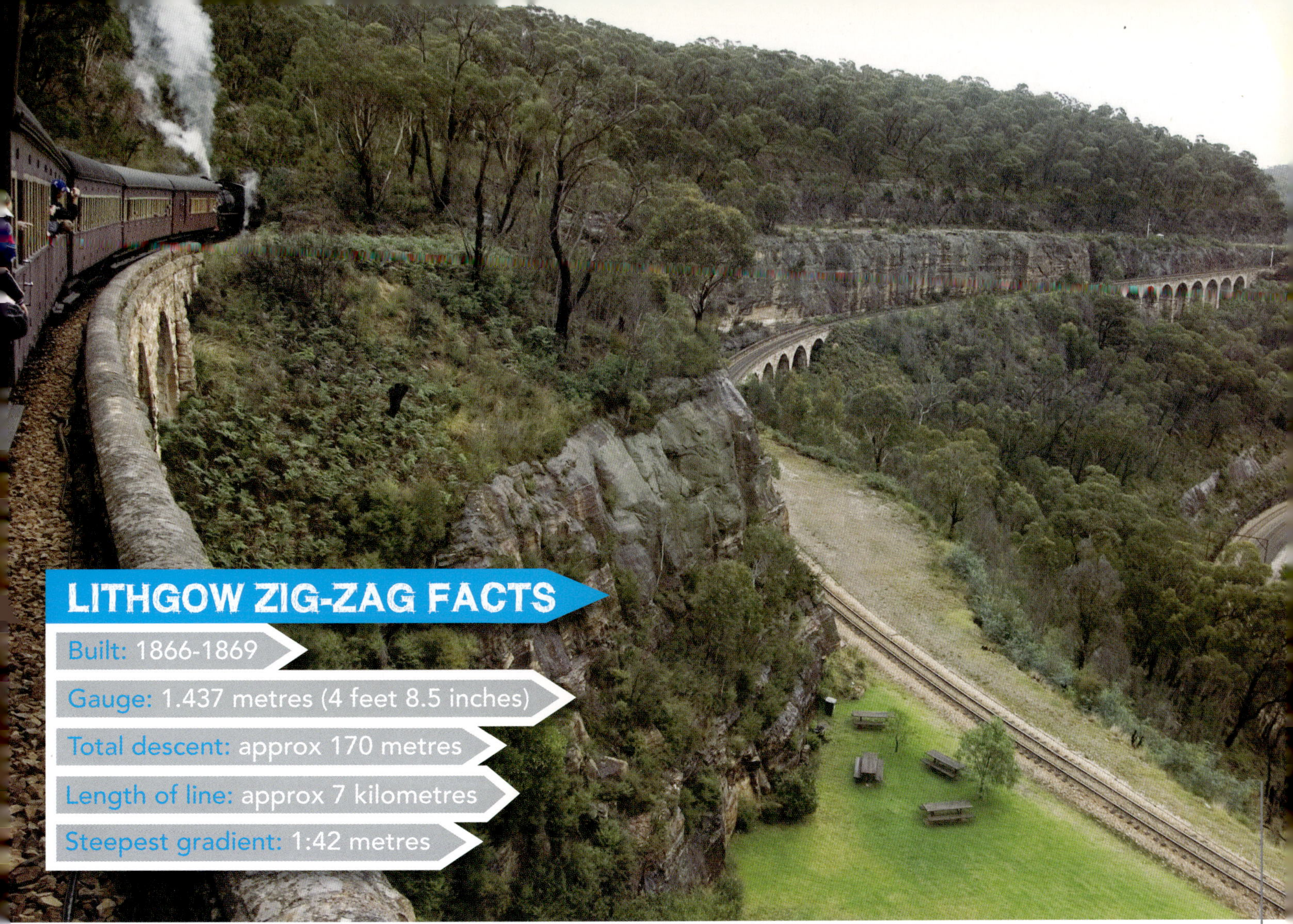

LITHGOW ZIG-ZAG FACTS

- Built: 1866-1869
- Gauge: 1.437 metres (4 feet 8.5 inches)
- Total descent: approx 170 metres
- Length of line: approx 7 kilometres
- Steepest gradient: 1:42 metres

DISUSE AND RESTORATION

By 1900, increased traffic on the line and the time taken for a train to pass the zig-zag section made it a bottleneck. In 1910, a new line bypassing the Zig-Zag line was built, and the original line fell into disuse. Ten tunnels had to be built through the mountain for the new line. During World War II, the long tunnel of the Zig-Zag was used to store ammunition. After the war it was used to grow mushrooms for a time. However, in 1972, railway buffs restored the original Zig-Zag section of the line. Today, it is a tourist attraction in the Blue Mountains.

GETTING THERE BY ROPE

Surveyors mapping the route of the Zig-Zag railway had to be lowered to the site on ropes from rocks above. Railway workers also had to be lowered during the early stages of construction.

Technology Time Machine! New Boiler Design

New boilers had to be designed for the steam engines running on the Zig-Zag Railway to enable them to cope with the steep gradient of the line. The boilers were designed to remain level during ascents and descents to keep them functioning efficiently. The new design was adopted for mountain steam engines throughout the world, particularly the USA.

The Central Australian Railway

The Central Australian Railway ran between Port Augusta and Alice Springs. It was built originally to transport coal from mines in Leigh Creek to Adelaide, and to provide rail transport between inland South Australian farming settlements and Adelaide, via Port Augusta.

The line was built in stages. The first section to Hawker was completed in 1880. In 1891, the line to Oodnadatta was finished, and the last stage to Alice Springs was completed in 1929.

THE ROUTE

Surveyors mapped and marked a route for the railway north from Port Augusta through wide sheep grazing plains, and on to the Flinders Ranges, winding its way through rocky valleys. From there it tracked through the mulga studded plains of the desert regions of the red centre of the continent, crossing the sandy landscapes to the west of Lake Eyre.

The Ghan's Route

CONSTRUCTION

Horse-drawn ploughs, scoops and graders and men with hand-tools prepared the ground for the base of the track. Dynamite was available for blasting rock cuttings through the Flinders Ranges section. But it was men with picks and shovels who did most of the back-breaking work, in weather that burned them up in the day and froze them at night.

LUGGING THE SLEEPERS

Men lifted the heavy timber sleepers from the flat-top wagons at the railhead. They loaded them across the backs of camels or onto wagons pulled by camels. Cameleers led the camels to where the sleepers were again lifted by hand into place across the bed of the track.

LAYING THE RAILS

Mechanical tracklayers were not available for the building of the first stages of the line, until it was extended from Oodnadatta to Alice Springs. Until then, steam-driven cranes lifted the heavy steel rails. But it was men who pushed them, balancing them on small trolleys along the completed line from rail stacks down-line from the railhead. And it was men who lifted them into place along the sleepers.

SLEEPER SLINGS

Railways workers working on the Central Australian Railway lifted and manipulated heavy timber sleepers using a small sling. It consisted of a loop of strong leather with a clasp handle attached to it, like that of suitcase handle. The sling was looped around the sleeper to enable the worker to lift it using one hand. Two workers could handle one sleeper in this way.

Camels and Cameleers

Before the railway from Oodnadatta to Alice Springs was built, goods were transported into central Australia by camels, led by Afghan cameleers. They were actually from Pakistan, but became known as Afghans, perhaps because they came from an area near Afghanistan. When the railway was built the camel trains stopped, and the South Australian Government ordered that all of the camels be shot. Not all were, and many escaped into desert where they successfully adapted and multiplied. Today, wild camel herds wander Central Australia. The Port Augusta to Alice Springs train became known as the Ghan after the Afghan cameleers.

Upgrading the Line

In 1979 an upgrade of the Central Australian Railway was completed. The narrow 1.068 metre gauge (3 feet 6 inches) line was replaced with the standard 1.437 metre gauge (4 feet 8.5 inches) to make it the same gauge as the main railway line it was connecting to.

RE-ROUTING THE LINE

From Port Augusta, the upgraded line shares the track as far as Tarcoola with the Trans-Australian Railway. From Tarcoola it turns northwards for Alice Springs via Maria in South Australia and Kulgera in the Northern Territory. The new route avoided the Flinders Ranges, which reduced construction costs. It also avoided the sandy landscapes to the west of Lake Eyre, reducing line maintenance greatly. Flooding along the old route frequently caused the bed of the track to be washed away, and other damage to the track. It also caused long delays, often leaving the trains stranded in the desert for days.

THE GHAN TRAIN

The upgraded line gave birth to the modern Ghan passenger train. The train was upgraded to luxury standard. It offers tourists a travel experience to make it one of the world's most spectacular desert train journeys.

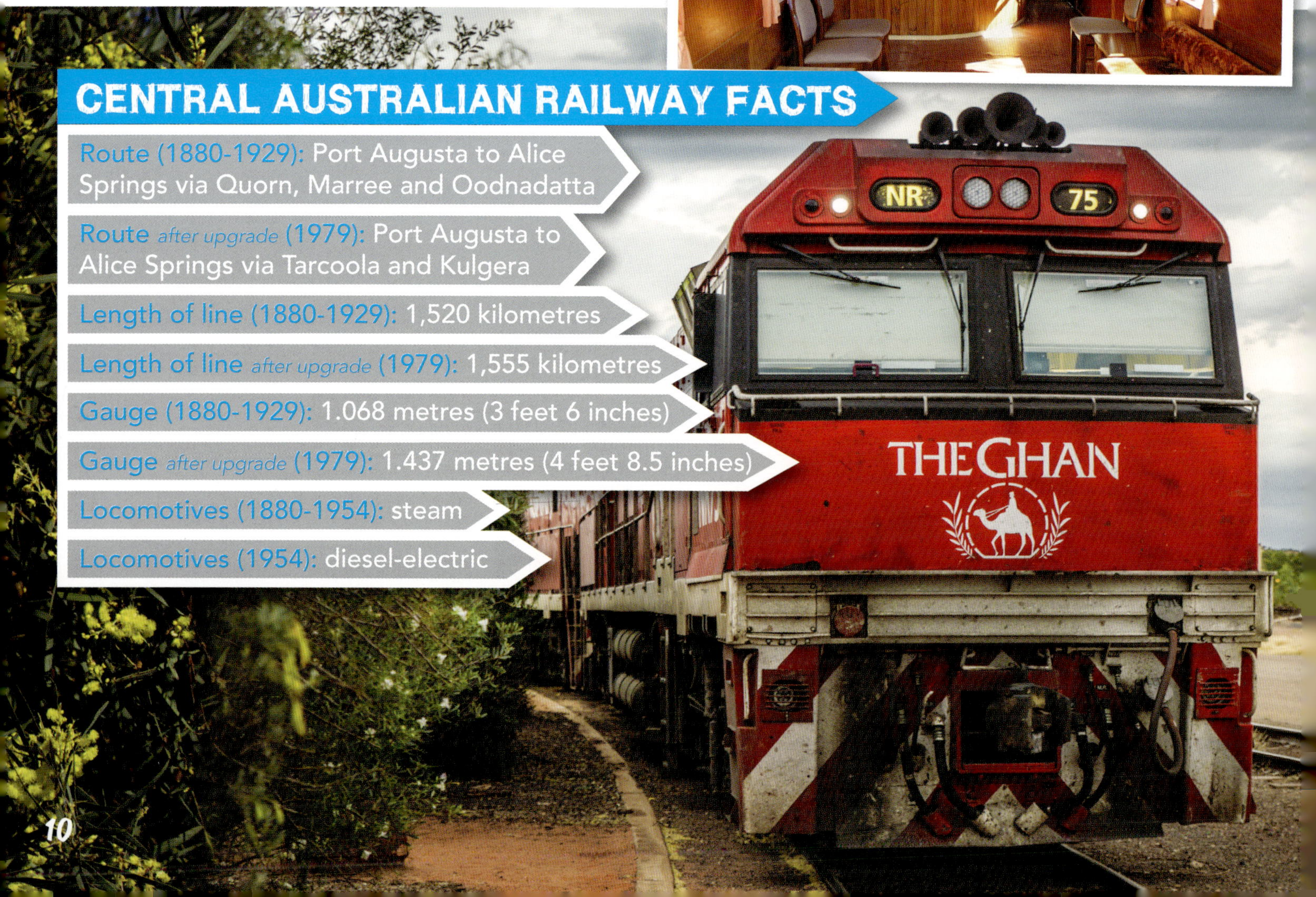

CENTRAL AUSTRALIAN RAILWAY FACTS

- **Route (1880-1929):** Port Augusta to Alice Springs via Quorn, Marree and Oodnadatta
- **Route *after upgrade* (1979):** Port Augusta to Alice Springs via Tarcoola and Kulgera
- **Length of line (1880-1929):** 1,520 kilometres
- **Length of line *after upgrade* (1979):** 1,555 kilometres
- **Gauge (1880-1929):** 1.068 metres (3 feet 6 inches)
- **Gauge *after upgrade* (1979):** 1.437 metres (4 feet 8.5 inches)
- **Locomotives (1880-1954):** steam
- **Locomotives (1954):** diesel-electric

The Locomotives

In 1954, the steam engines that hauled the trains were replaced by diesel-electric locomotives. The diesel-electric locomotives use diesel fuel to drive generators that produce electricity to power electric engines. They are more efficient than steam engines, not needing to take on water along the route, and not needing their boilers continually stoked with coal, or fed with oil. By 1954, a train ran twice a week between Adelaide and Alice Springs. It was a mixed train, carrying both goods and passengers. It took 42.5 hours to make the 1,555 kilometre trip.

THE DREAM OF A TRANSCONTINENTAL CROSSING

The upgrading of the line to Alice Springs was not the end of the Central Australian Railway story. Since 1929 it had always been the dream of the South Australian politicians and railway planners to extend the line from Alice Springs to Darwin, to build a transcontinental railway from south to north through Australia's centre. It would be 74 years after the first steam train arrived at Alice Springs in 1929, before the first diesel-electric locomotive powered into Darwin, in 2003.

Concrete Sleepers

Concrete sleepers are heavier than sleepers made from timber, and tracks built with concrete sleepers are more stable than those built with timber sleepers. Concrete sleepers are made with steel clip-holders embedded in them, one on either side of where the steel rail will sit. Curved steel clips are driven through the holders, using sledgehammers. The curved part of the clip overlaps the flat, base part of the rail to firmly clamp the rail to the sleeper. This anchors the rails much more firmly to the sleepers than do the spikes hammered into timber sleepers. Concrete sleepers reduce railway maintenance, as they are more durable than timber, and cannot be attacked by termites.

Extending the Line

Work on the Central Australian Railway from Alice Springs to Darwin began in July 2001, and was scheduled for completion in April 2004. It was finished in September 2003, seven months ahead of schedule.

PREPARING FOR CONSTRUCTION

Track-laying depots to store materials and construction equipment were set up at the towns of Tennant Creek and Katherine. The Aboriginal owners of the land agreed to the route. Sacred sites near the line were fenced for protection during construction.

ACROSS THE DESERT

From Tennant Creek, the line was laid south to Alice Springs and north towards Katherine. From Katherine, construction proceeded north to Darwin and south to meet the line coming north from Tennant Creek. The two ends of the section were joined on 13 September 2002.

STEEL

The steel for the line was smelted and the rails fabricated at the Whyalla Steelworks in South Australia. Road trains transported it north to the Tennant Creek and Katherine depots. From there the rails were transported on the completed tracks to the railheads.

Freight Trains

The line to Alice Springs was extended to Darwin mainly for the purpose of transporting goods from southern Australia to Darwin, Australia's gateway port to Asia. The first freight train left Adelaide for Darwin on 15 January 2004.

THE SLEEPER FACTORIES

Factories were built at Tennant Creek and Katherine to produce the concrete sleepers. The Tennant Creek factory employed 60 people and produced approximately 1.1 million sleepers. At Katherine, 40 workers produced approximately one million sleepers.

BALLAST QUARRIES

Huge amounts of ballast were needed to make a stable base for the sleepers. During each work shift 3,000 tonnes of ballast were laid. At Tennant Creek, 1.55 million tonnes of rock were crushed. Fifty wagons were trucked to Tennant Creek by road to carry the ballast out along the newly laid line to the railhead. At the Katherine ballast works, 1.3 million tonnes of rock were crushed and delivered to the work site in the same way.

A SMOOTH RIDE

From Whyalla, the rails were transported north in 27.5 metre lengths. At the work site they were welded into 357.5 metre lengths. When laid, these were then welded together. This made a continuous rail from Alice Springs to Darwin, providing a smooth ride for passengers, with none of the noise wheels make when they cross rails with expansion gaps in them.

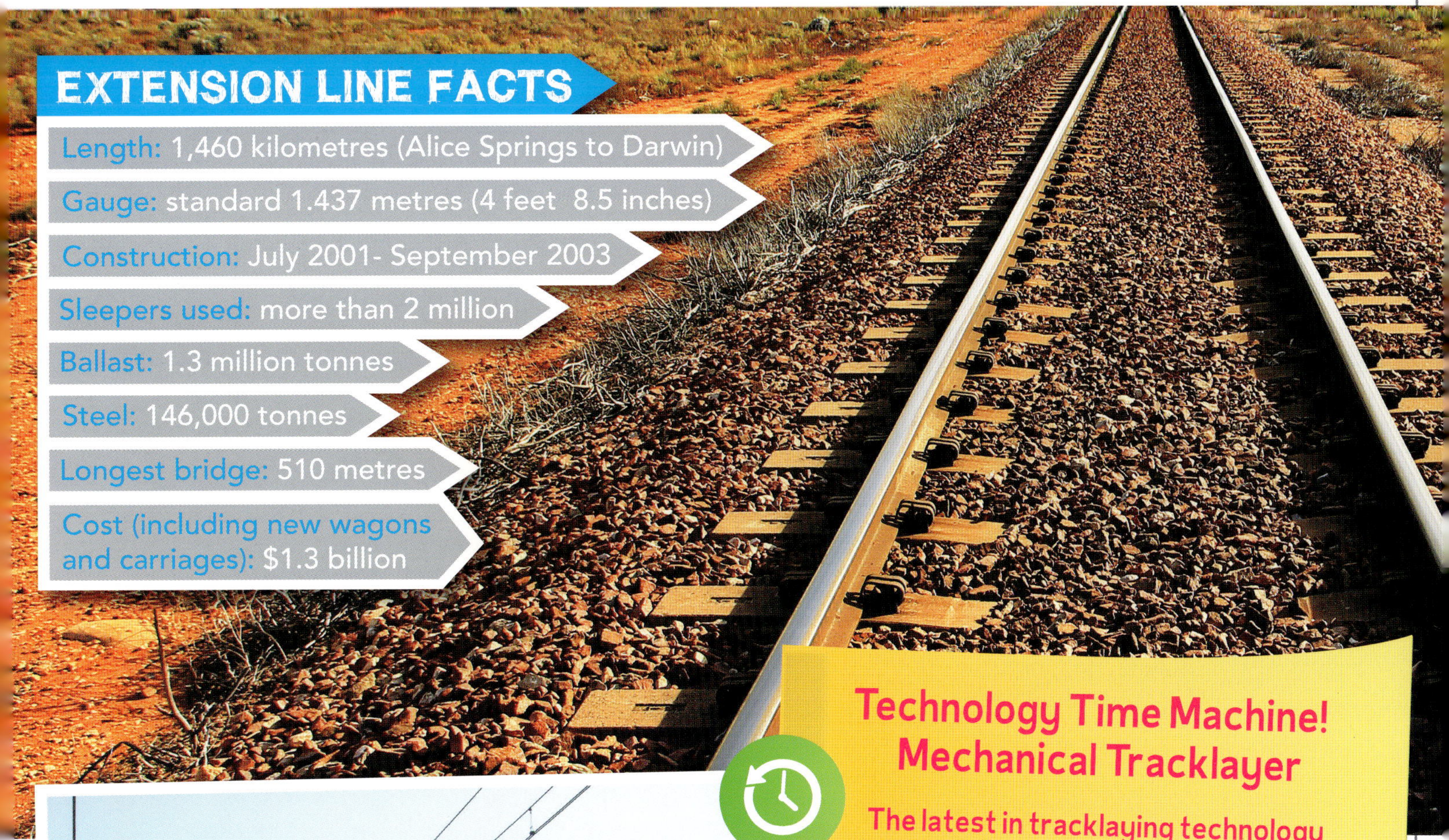

EXTENSION LINE FACTS

- Length: 1,460 kilometres (Alice Springs to Darwin)
- Gauge: standard 1.437 metres (4 feet 8.5 inches)
- Construction: July 2001- September 2003
- Sleepers used: more than 2 million
- Ballast: 1.3 million tonnes
- Steel: 146,000 tonnes
- Longest bridge: 510 metres
- Cost (including new wagons and carriages): $1.3 billion

Technology Time Machine! Mechanical Tracklayer

The latest in tracklaying technology was used on the Central Australian Railway extension to Darwin. A huge machine resembling a giant caterpillar carrying a load of sleepers crept above the path of the track from the railhead. As it moved it picked up the sleepers from its inside and laid them across the track's path. Then it would return to the railhead and drag lengths of steel rail from flat-top wagons sitting on the completed line, and lay them in place along the sleepers. Railway workers would then fix the rails in place by driving clips into steel holders embedded in the sleepers using sledge hammers.

The West Coast Wilderness Railway

Tasmania's West Coast Wilderness Railway was built by the Mt Lyell Company in 1889 to transport ore from its copper mine at Queenstown through the mountainous wilderness of Tasmania's west coast to the seaport of Strahan. The line closed in 1963 when the road between the two towns was upgraded. However, in 1999, the Federal Government granted the Tasmanian Government $20.4 million to restore the line.

In February 2013 the Federal Group announced that the railway was no longer viable and it would be terminating its lease. Following track work, the railway re-opened in 2014 and is operated by the Abt Railway Ministerial Corporation, a State Government corporation.

It now operates as the West Coast Wilderness Railway, and is one of the world's most scenic tourist railways.

A SPECTACULAR ROUTE

The line rises steeply from near Queenstown through rainforest to high above the gorge of King River. It then descends spectacularly along the edge of the gorge to the broad banks of the river, which it follows into Strahan. A number of trestle bridges were built to carry the line back and forth across the river.

AN ENGINEERING CHALLENGE

The steepness of the terrain across which the railway was to pass posed a serious problem for the railway engineers. No locomotive could ascend and descend the steep slopes along the proposed route. The engineers solved the problem by using a rack and pinion traction system. The locomotive has a cog wheel that locks onto pinions (teeth) along a rack laid between the rails. This enables the locomotive to haul the train up the steep ascent, and stops it running out of control when it is descending. In the early years of the railway, a second locomotive was shunted from a siding to push the train from behind up the steepest slope.

DR ROMAN ABT

The rack and pinion traction system used on the Mt Lyell company's railway had only been recently invented by Swiss engineer Dr Roman Abt. Railway engineers now call the system by his name: ABT.

Rack and pinion traction system

WORKING CONDITIONS

Construction took two years. Man power and horsepower built the line. The track path had to be cut through dense rainforest along the steep sides of the King River Gorge by men using handsaws, picks and shovels. Timber workers cut timber for the bridges. Conditions for the workers were very difficult. They battled rain, constant dampness, leeches and poisonous snakes. And they had no adequate clothing for the cold and wet.

WEST COAST WILDERNESS RAILWAY FACTS

- Constructed: 1889
- Gauge: 1.068 metres (3 feet 6 inches)
- Length of line: 35 kilometres
- Number of bridges: 40
- Steepest gradient: 4.25 metres per 100 metres

The Trans-Australian Railway

The Trans-Australian Railway in its day was regarded as an engineering miracle. It was a 1,680 kilometre track across the desert, with no road access, linking Kalgoorlie in Western Australia to Port Augusta in South Australia. Work began in 1913 and was finished in record time in 1917. The line connected Western Australia with eastern states. Before the railway, the only transport link was by sea. With the existing lines from Port Augusta to Adelaide, the new line made a continuous rail link from Perth to Adelaide.

MAKING THE WAY

Surveyors mapped a course for the track, taking into account the terrain it would have to pass through. They measured the varying height of the land above sea level to establish the levels and gradients needed for the track. Geologists were part of the survey teams. They drilled shafts to test the composition of the soils and rocks below the surface of the proposed route to ensure the track would rest on a stable base.

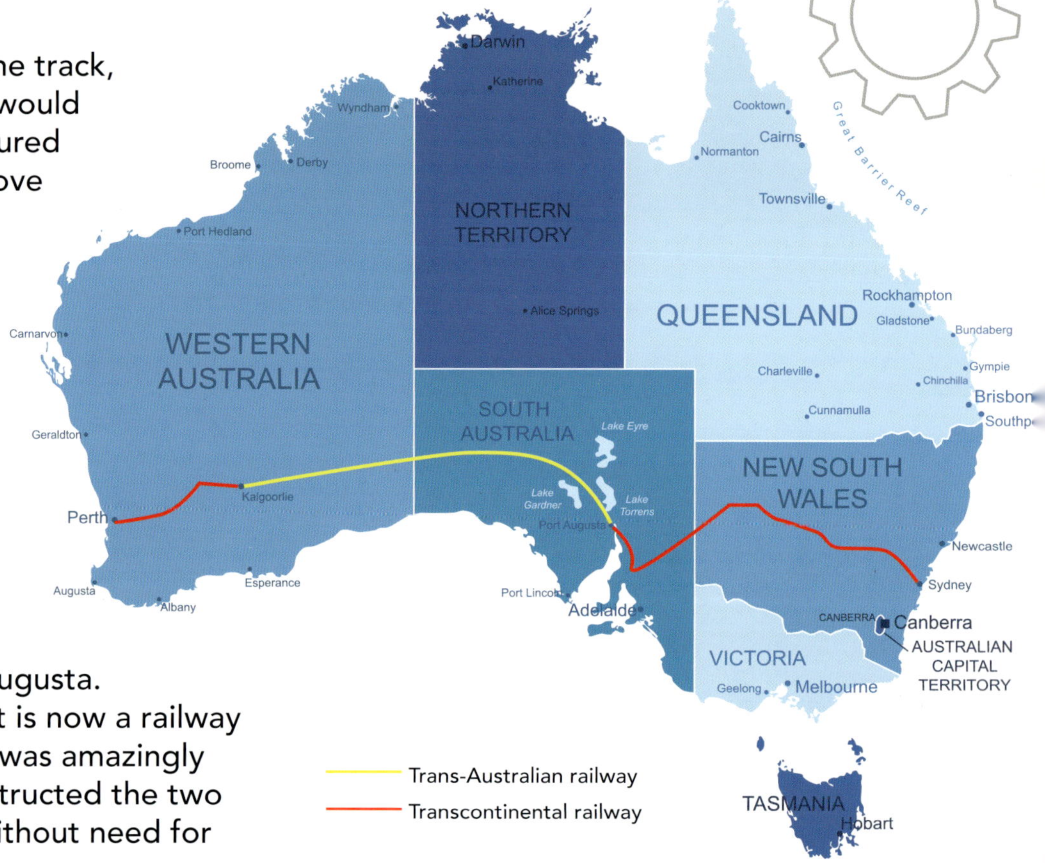

Two teams of surveyors worked independently. One worked from Kalgoorlie, the other from Port Augusta. The two teams finally met at what is now a railway siding at Ooldea, SA. The survey was amazingly accurate. When the line was constructed the two ends came together at Ooldea without need for any late changes of direction.

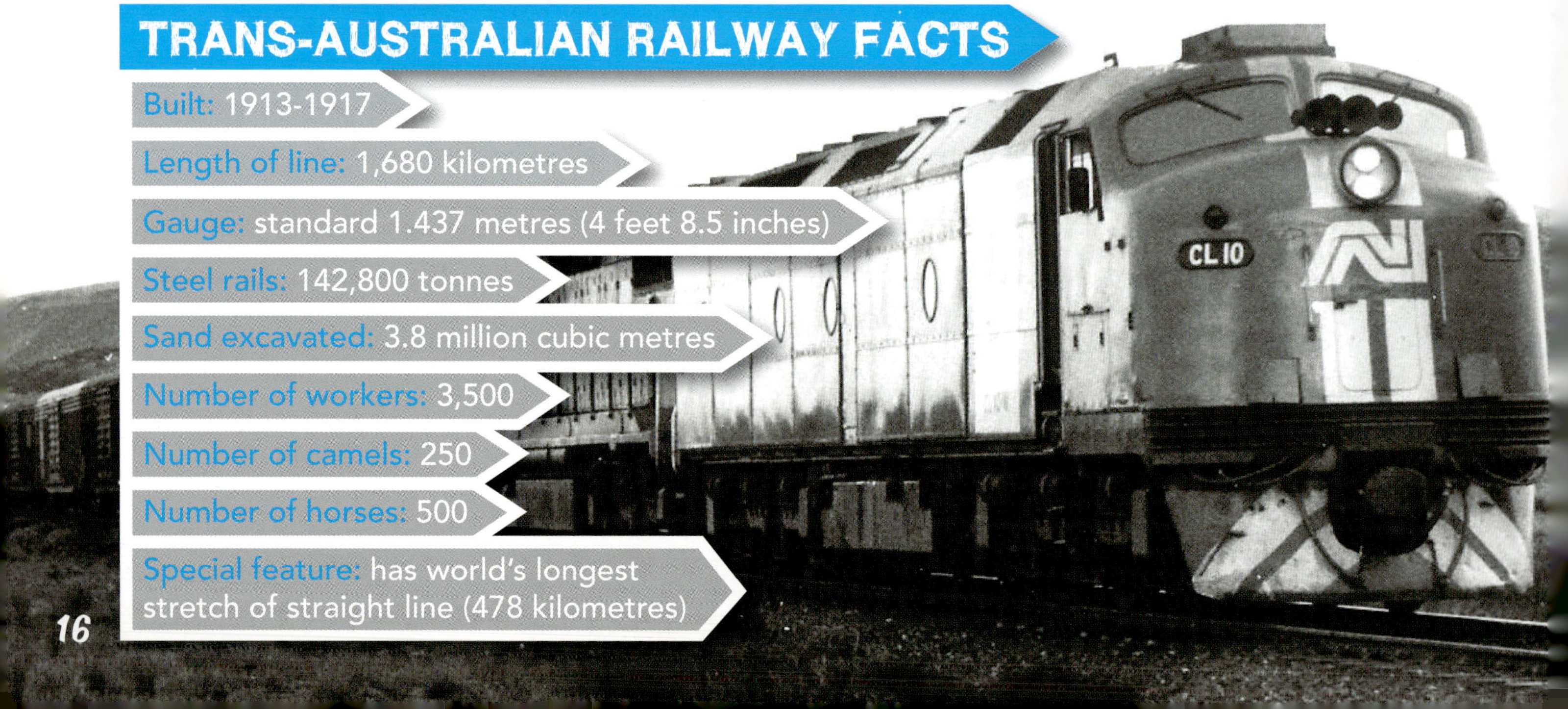

TRANS-AUSTRALIAN RAILWAY FACTS

- **Built:** 1913-1917
- **Length of line:** 1,680 kilometres
- **Gauge:** standard 1.437 metres (4 feet 8.5 inches)
- **Steel rails:** 142,800 tonnes
- **Sand excavated:** 3.8 million cubic metres
- **Number of workers:** 3,500
- **Number of camels:** 250
- **Number of horses:** 500
- **Special feature:** has world's longest stretch of straight line (478 kilometres)

CAMELS

Camels were used to haul wagons carrying water tanks, food and equipment across the dry plains of the Nullarbor to the surveying teams. As the surveyors mapped the route, two teams of camels dragging heavy chains cut a swathe through sand and vegetation to mark it for the construction teams.

A FEDERAL AGREEMENT

The rail line was built as the result of an agreement that had been made between the colony of Western Australia and the other Australian colonies in the lead up to Federation. Western Australia had agreed to join the Federation of the Australian colonies to form the Commonwealth of Australia in 1901. But it agreed only on the condition that the new Federal Government build a rail line between Kalgoorlie and Port Augusta to link Western Australia with eastern states.

Moving Towns

There were no towns built along the entire length of the route. Temporary work camps were set up in the desert, and then moved as the line progressed. They were like small towns, with temporary boarding houses for workers. A shop, a hospital and a post office were set up in railway carriages parked on the completed track near the railhead.

Technology Time Machine! The First Mechanical Tracklayer

Mechanical tracklayers were first used in Australia on the construction of the Trans-Australian Railway. The tracklayer was a flat-top wagon carrying a steam-driven crane and winch. It was linked to a number of flat-top wagons carrying 27 metre lengths of rail behind. The flat-top wagon was pushed from behind along the completed line to the railhead by a steam locomotive. The winch hauled a length of rail forward onto the tracklayer. The rail was then lifted by the crane, and swung into place on the sleepers, guided by the navvies (railway construction workers).

Construction in the Desert

WATER SUPPLY

Once construction began, a reliable supply of water had to be provided for the 3,500 construction workers and the 750 camels and horses. Steam locomotives and the other steam-driven machinery working at the railhead also had to be supplied with water. Small dams were built near Kalgoorlie and Port Augusta to catch and store rainwater. Across the great expanse of the Nullarbor Plain, 27 bores had to be sunk.

Tracklayer laying the TransAustralian Railway

EARTHWORKS

Across most of the 800 kilometres of the flat Nullarbor Plain no major earthworks were needed, but through sandy country at the western section cuttings had to be constructed through sand hills and rocky country. Men dug out cuttings using picks and shovels. Steam-driven shovels and horse-drawn scrapers and scoops were used to remove sand and gravel. Camel-drawn ploughs broke up gravelly sections ready for scrapers. In one 50 kilometre section nearly one million cubic metres of sand were moved.

LAYING THE SLEEPERS

The track was built into the desert from both Port Augusta and Kalgoorlie. As the new lines progressed, steam trains hauled equipment and materials to the railheads along the newly completed lines. The wooden sleepers were lifted by hand and strapped to frames harnessed to the backs of camels, six at a time. The camels carried them forward from the railhead to where workers lifted them into place on the levelled path of the track.

Port Augusta

Port Augusta was turned from a small, sleepy settlement into a thriving railway town. Railway sheds, factories and workshops were built as well as an impressive new station.

RAILS AND BALLAST

The steel rails, each 27 metres long, were lifted from the flat-top wagons by a steam-driven crane, and fixed to the sleepers. Crushed rock ballast was brought by rail from quarries at Woocalla, 122 kilometres north-west of Port Augusta. It was tipped from the railway wagons and spread between the sleepers to provide the stability needed to prevent the tracks moving sideways.

Technology Time Machine! Fixing the Rails in Place

The rails were fixed to the sleepers by steel spikes, called dog spikes, driven in by hand by railway workers using sledgehammers. The flat top of the spike overlapped the flat, base part of the rail, holding it down. There was one spike on each side of the rail at each sleeper.

Joining the Rails

Lengths of rail were joined to form a continuous line with steel flat plates bolted to the sides of the rails. Between each joint a small expansion gap of approximately two centimetres was left to allow the line to expand and contract with the extreme changes in desert temperatures. Without the expansion joint the rails would have buckled.

THE TRANS-AUSTRALIAN TODAY

When it was finished in 1917, the Trans-Australian Railway completed a continuous rail link between Perth and Sydney, via Adelaide and Melbourne. However, because a number of different railways with different gauges made up the complete journey, passengers had to change trains five times: at Kalgoorlie, Port Augusta, Adelaide, Melbourne and Albury.

Today, the Trans-Australian Railway is part of a continuous, standard gauge line (1.437 metres, or 4 feet 8.5 inches) between Sydney and Perth, via Broken Hill and Adelaide. It carries the luxury tourist train, the Indian Pacific.

Melbourne City Loop

Until 1981, ninety per cent of all passengers travelling to the city of Melbourne by train finished their journey at Flinders Street Station, which is situated on the southern edge of the city centre. This meant that people who worked at the northern and eastern ends of the city had to either walk or catch a tram to their workplace. At that time, Flinders Street was one of the busiest railway stations in the world, with more than one train leaving every minute during peak periods.

THE FIRST SOD

On 22 June 1971, the construction of an underground line began with the turning of the first sod near the Flinders Street Station signal box. Trains began operating through the loop in 1981, and the project was fully completed in 1985. The City Loop meant that passengers could enter the city at one of three underground stations at the eastern and northern ends of the city centre. Flinders Street Station is still one of the world's busiest, but now not all passengers arriving at and leaving the city have to use it.

Station Names

Parliament Station was named after Victoria's Parliament buildings that are located above it. Museum Station was named after the old Melbourne Museum. When the museum was moved to Carlton the station was re-named Melbourne Central after the shopping complex that is built above it. Flagstaff Station is named after the Flagstaff Gardens above it.

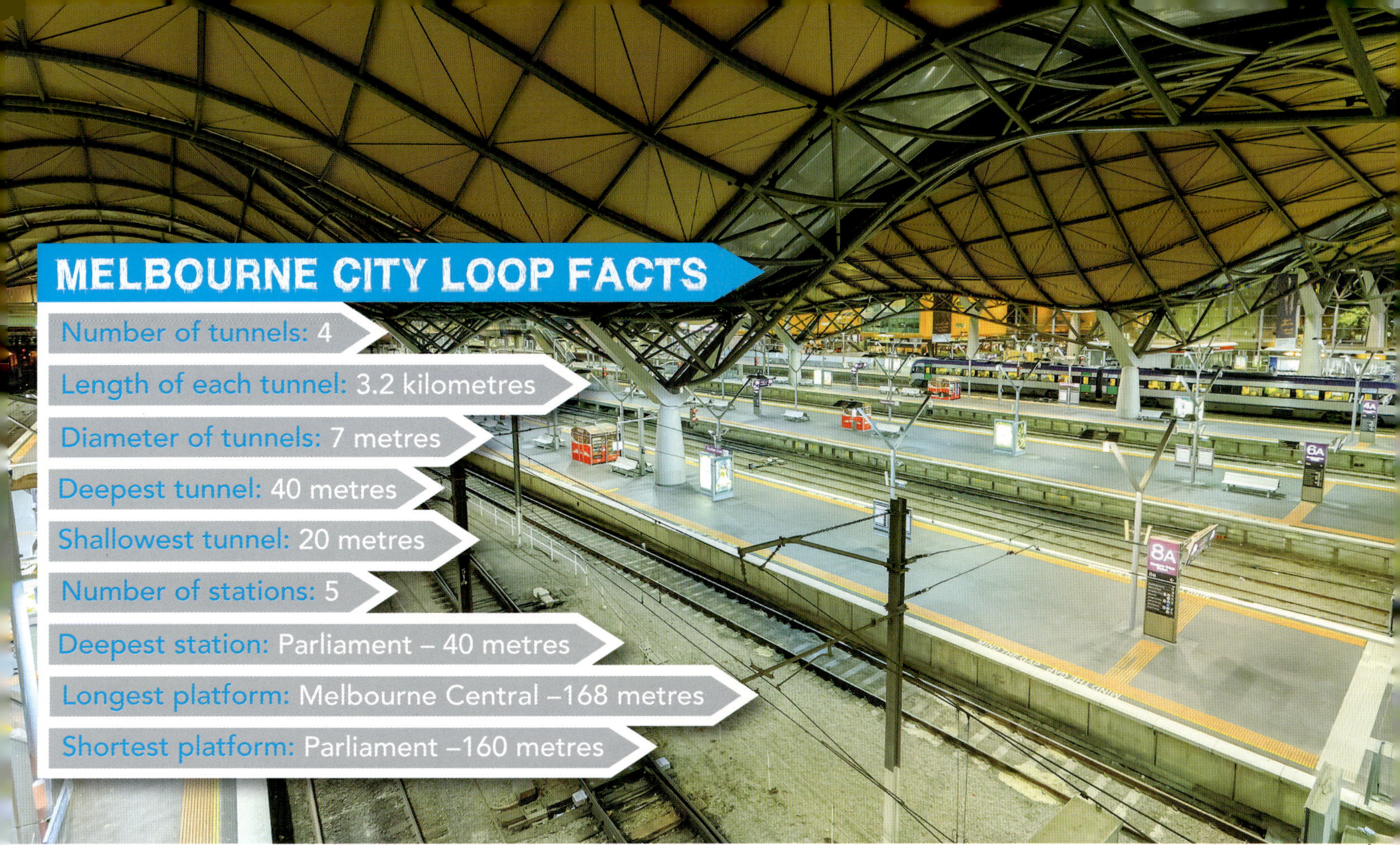

MELBOURNE CITY LOOP FACTS

- **Number of tunnels:** 4
- **Length of each tunnel:** 3.2 kilometres
- **Diameter of tunnels:** 7 metres
- **Deepest tunnel:** 40 metres
- **Shallowest tunnel:** 20 metres
- **Number of stations:** 5
- **Deepest station:** Parliament – 40 metres
- **Longest platform:** Melbourne Central –168 metres
- **Shortest platform:** Parliament –160 metres

AN UNDERGROUND CIRCUIT

The Melbourne City Loop is a circuit of four rail lines running deep beneath Melbourne's CBD (Central Business District). There are tunnels at two levels, and at each level there are two parallel tunnels, each with one track. There are three underground stations: Parliament, Melbourne Central and Flagstaff. Each station has platforms in the two tunnels. The three underground stations and the surface stations, Flinders Street and Southern Cross (Spencer Street), make a loop of stations on the border of Melbourne's Central Business District.

The Underground station concourses are located just below the surface. At these are ticket windows and machines where passengers can buy tickets before descending by escalators, or lifts, to the two levels of platforms below.

The Loop tracks descend underground to the east of Flinders Street Station, and emerge near Southern Cross Station to the west. There are also tunnels connecting the Loop to surface lines near the Richmond, Jolimont and North Melbourne stations. The complete system connects to the 15 lines that radiate from central Melbourne to the city's inner and outer suburbs.

Constructing the Loop

Constructing the Loop involved excavating two tunnels, each 3.2 kilometres long, and up to 40 metres below ground. Tunnelling work had to be carried out without affecting the buildings of the city above.

PREPARATIONS

Computer programs were used to assist engineers to write the complex specifications and draw plans for the many elements that make up the Loop system: the exact routes and levels of the tunnels, the tracks, stations, lighting, and signalling and customer information systems.

Before construction of the tunnels could begin, exploratory shafts were sunk from the streets above to test how the rock and clay layers would react to tunnelling. These tests gave the engineers the information they needed to make small adjustments to route directions and levels. This explains why the tunnels undulate slightly and the stations are not at the same level.

PILOT TUNNELS

Narrow pilot tunnels were constructed first along the proposed paths of the four tunnels. The pilot tunnels gave the engineers practical knowledge of the rock and soils that the larger tunnels would be bored through. They paved the way for the much larger boring machines.

Technology Time Machine! Tunnel Construction

Tunnels can be constructed in two ways. The path of the tunnel can be excavated from above. The tunnel is then built and covered. This is called the 'cut and cover method'. Or the tunnel space can be bored through the underground by huge augers, and the tunnel walls and floor built in that space. This is called the 'driven' method.

BORING THE TUNNELS

The approaches to the tunnels were excavated first. These consisted of an open ramp leading to a rectangular tunnel that descended to the circular tunnels below. They were excavated from the surface, built, and then the rectangular tunnel section was covered. Huge boring machines called augers gouged out the circular tunnels of the Loop. They followed the pilot tunnels through the rock and clay layers. During excavation of the Loop tunnels a total of 900,000 cubic metres of rock and soil were removed. Thirty thousand tonnes of steel reinforcement was used to strengthen the 300,000 cubic metres of concrete used in the construction.

A DESIGN CHALLENGE

When the Loop engineers began construction of Flagstaff Station they discovered a layer of compacted clay between the upper and lower tunnels. This clay band was not strong enough to support the upper platforms of the station. The problem was solved by boring holes upwards from the rock below beside the lower track tunnels. Into these were built columns upwards from below to support the upper platforms of the station.

THE STATIONS

The Upper levels of the three stations and their concourses were built after huge volumes of rock and clay were excavated from the surface. The areas were then covered as building progressed.

Loop Technology

When it was built, Melbourne's Loop contained the latest in train management technology.

WORLD'S LARGEST

The signalling system was fully integrated by computer with the inner city surface lines that connect with the Loop. The computerised signal system was, at that time, the world's largest computer-based train control and management system.

DEPARTURE INFORMATION

All station platforms had monitors displaying information about the next scheduled train, its departure time and the stations it would stop at. Today, the monitors also tell passengers how long they have to wait for the next train.

Technology Time Machine! Reducing Noise

To reduce the high levels of noise that trains make in confined spaces, the tunnel walls of the Loop were fitted with acoustic pods to absorb sound and reduce the amount of train noise that would reverberate in the tunnels. The acoustic pods are long tubes of perforated metal that are filled with fibres. Sound enters the tubes through the perforations (holes) and is absorbed by the fibres. There are four acoustic pods fitted along the length of each tunnel.

Engineers also designed a floating track structure, consisting of a double layer of sleepers that reduced the strength of the vibrations of the train wheels reaching the tunnel floor. This lowered the rumbling noise of passing trains that would have been heard in the buildings above.

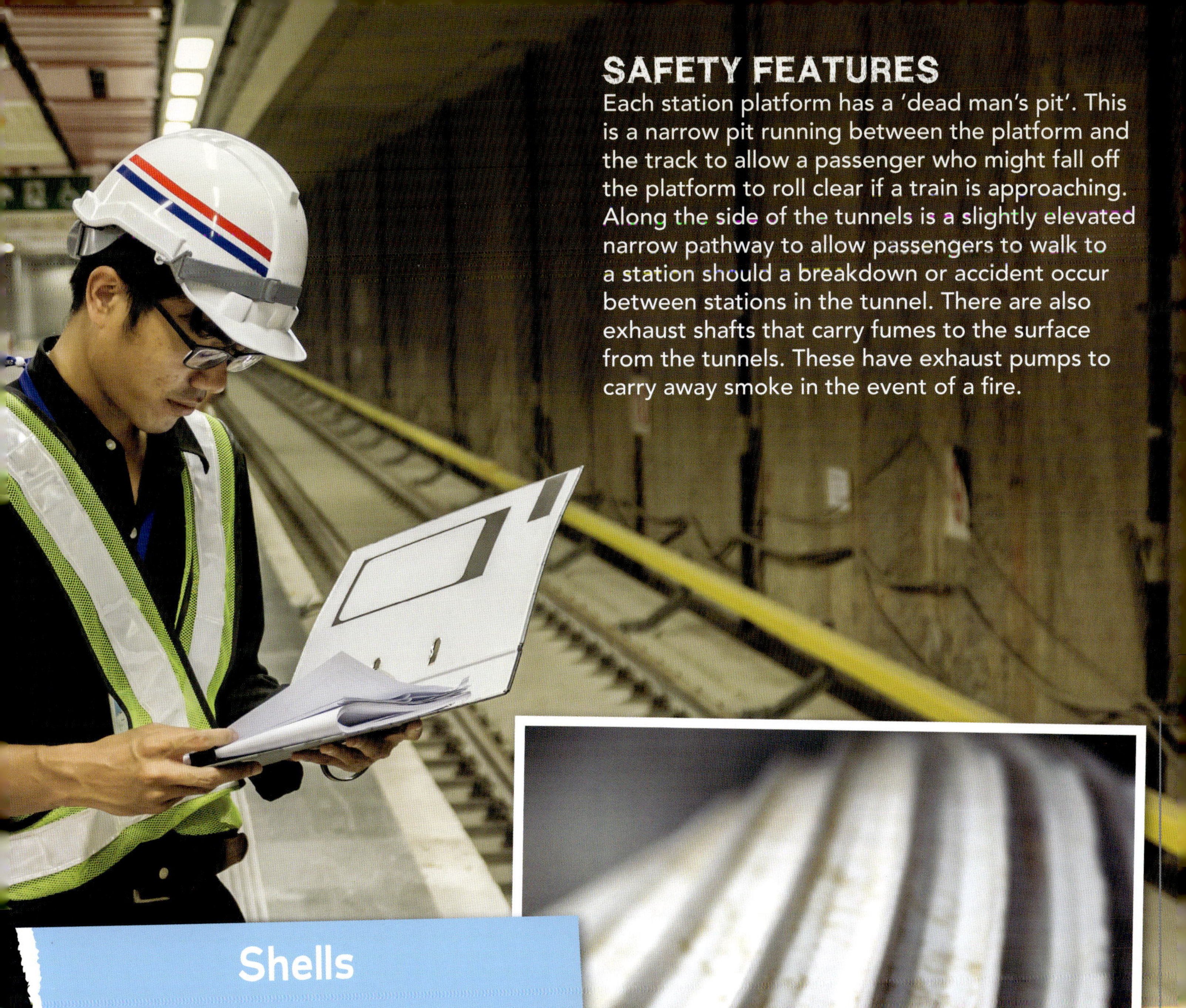

SAFETY FEATURES

Each station platform has a 'dead man's pit'. This is a narrow pit running between the platform and the track to allow a passenger who might fall off the platform to roll clear if a train is approaching. Along the side of the tunnels is a slightly elevated narrow pathway to allow passengers to walk to a station should a breakdown or accident occur between stations in the tunnel. There are also exhaust shafts that carry fumes to the surface from the tunnels. These have exhaust pumps to carry away smoke in the event of a fire.

Shells

During excavation of the Loop exit tunnel near the North Melbourne Station, excavators uncovered shells 8,000 years old. This revealed that the area was seabed thousands of years ago. Carbon dating techniques revealed the age of the shells.

HOW THE TRAINS RUN

Train services run through the loop in one direction, or both, depending on the time of day and the day of the week.

Queensland Tilt Train

When it began operation in 1998, the Queensland Tilt train was the fastest train travelling on a narrow 1.067 metre gauge (3 feet 6 inches) line.

The Tilt Train began operating between Brisbane and Rockhampton in 1998. It ran on the existing line between Brisbane and Rockhampton. Before services began, the track was upgraded giving it much heavier steel rails.

Technology of the Time! Passive and Active Tilting

Some tilting trains are constructed so that the forces acting on the carriages during a change of direction cause the tilting. This is called a passive tilt. Other trains have a computer-controlled device that activates the tilting mechanism. This is called an active tilt. The Queensland Tilt Train is an active tilt train.

EXTENSION AND A NEW TRAIN

Electric locomotives hauled the first Tilt Train, drawing power from overhead electricity lines. In 2003, the service was extended to Cairns, and the locomotives were changed to diesel power. New carriages were built at railway workshops in Maryborough. The Tilt Train has two locomotive carriages, one pulling from the front and one pushing from behind with a total of five sitting cars, a luggage van and a club car.

QUEENSLAND TILT TRAIN FACTS

- **Gauge:** 1.067 m (3 feet 6 inches)
- **Length of line:** 1,681 kilometres (Brisbane to Cairns)
- **Travelling time:** 24 hours 55 minutes

WHY THE TILT?

When a fast-moving vehicle turns, forces act on it to make it and its passengers continue in the direction of the vehicle before it turned. Passengers in a fast train taking a bend feel a force on them that makes them lean against the turn to prevent themselves from falling over. This force can cause a train to derail if it is taking a bend too fast. A titling train reduces this force. The carriages of the Queensland Tilt Train lean at an angle of five degrees into the direction of the turn to reduce the force on the train and the people inside. This allows the train to take the bend at a faster speed than it could otherwise, and for its passengers not to feel pressed into the sides of their seats or luggage to move about on the floor or in luggage compartments.

DERAILMENT

The Queensland Tilt Train derailed near Cairns on 15 November 2004. It is thought the track was not stable enough to take the weight and forces of the train travelling at high speed. A number of safety changes have been implemented since the 2004 crash, which include:

- the installation of Automatic Train Protection (ATP) technology on all Tilt Train services, which monitors driver action and controls the speed of the train
- improved emergency equipment, lighting and signage
- upgraded trackside equipment and indicator boards
- dedicated phone numbers for emergency services to contact Queensland Rail
- safety briefings for passengers was reviewed and extra emergency training was given to on-board staff
- Overhauling of The Tilt Train fleet

Railways at a Glance

Central Australian Railway - The Ghan. Travels 1,460 km between Alice Springs and Darwin, constructed between 2001-2003

Central Australian Railway - The Ghan. Travels 1,555 km between Port Augusta and Alice Springs, constructed between 1880-1929

Queensand Tilt Train. Travels 1,681 km between Brisbane and Cairns, constructed between 1998-2003

Lithgow Zig-Zag Railway. Travels 7 km from Lithgow across the Blue Mountains, constructed between 1866-1869

Trans-Australian Railway - The Indian Pacific. Travels 1,680 km between Kalgoorlie (WA) and Port Augusta (SA), constructed between 1913-1917

West Coast Wilderness Railway. Travels 35 km between Queenstown and Strahan (Tas), constructed in 1889

Melbourne City Loop. Travels 3.2 km within Melbourne City, constructed between 1971-1985

Railways Snapshot

KURANDA SCENIC RAILWAY QUEENSLAND

The Kuranda line was built in 1886 to serve the inland mining town of Herberton. From the coastal plain near Cairns, the railway climbs 300 metres along the gorge of the Barron River. It now terminates at the tourist town of Kuranda. Along its route it passes through 15 tunnels and crosses 36 bridges. At the long trestle bridge across Stoney Creek Falls, it stops to allow passengers to take in and photograph the spectacular scenery.

Route: Cairns to Kuranda
Distance: 34 kilometres
Duration: 1 hour 45 minutes

The Prospector runs between Perth and the gold-mining town of Kalgoorlie. When the first Prospector ran in 1971, it was the fastest train in Australia, reaching speeds of 120 kilometres per hour.

THE ADELAIDE TO MELBOURNE OVERLAND

The Overland linked Adelaide and Melbourne in 1887 on 1.6 metre (5 feet 3.5 inches) gauge line. It now runs on a standard 1.437 metre gauge (4 feet 8.5 inches) track. The Overland was named after adventurous pioneers of the nineteenth century who trekked overland across the Australian continent and became known as the Overlanders.

THE GULFLANDER QUEENSLAND

The Heritage Listed Normanton to Croydon line was never connected to the state rail network and remains the only line in Queensland still measured in miles. The journey is often described as "going from nowhere to nowhere", but actually the train takes passengers through stunning savannah territories.

Route: Normanton to Croydon
Distance 152 kilometres
Duration: 5 hours

The XPT (Express Passenger Train) was introduced in 1982. It reaches speeds of 160 kilometres per hour on a normal trip, but is capable of faster speeds. Until 1999, the XPT held the Australian speed record for a train - 193 kilometres per hour. The XPT is used on services between Sydney and Brisbane, Melbourne, Dubbo and Murwillumbah.

PUFFING BILLY VICTORIA

Puffing Billy is a tourist steam train running from Belgrave to Gembrook in the Dandenong Ranges east of Melbourne. The line, at 24.5 kilometres long, runs through a mixture of rainforest and open farmland. The train runs on the original 0.76 metre (2 feet 6 inches) track that was opened in December 1900. It is one of Melbourne's most popular tourist attractions, running twice daily both ways, except on Christmas Day.

The Future of Rail in Australia

In the future it is possible that Australia will have a train network that offers faster travel. In Europe, Japan, South Korea and China, trains that travel almost as fast as airplanes link many cities. In Japan, bullet trains have a system of magnets that hold them just above the rails. With minimal friction they travel very fast, very quietly and very smoothly. It is possible that in the future similar trains will travel between Australian cities. These trains will compete with airlines for intercity passengers.

The current proposal is for a High Speed Rail (HSR) between Brisbane-Sydney-Canberra-Melbourne, with numerous regional stops along the way. It would take less than three hours to travel between Sydney and Melbourne, and Sydney and Brisbane. It could carry 84 million passengers a year. However current predictions for this train being operational are for 2065.

Glossary

aneroid barometer a surveying device that allows surveyors to accurately measure heights in rugged countryside

ballast crushed rock used as a base

bogeys the set of wheels of a railway carriage or wagon

cameleers persons who drive camels as a form of transport

carbon dating scientific method of determining the age of an object by examining the state of the carbon in it

concourses large open areas across which people move

diesel-electric a locomotive that uses diesel fuel to power motors that generate the electricity that drives the engine

embankment a bank constructed along the side of a hill, or river, to provide a path for a railway or road

expansion gaps gaps in a steel rail to allow it to expand when heated

flange a rim that keeps a wheel in place, stopping it from sliding off the rail

flat-top wagon a railway wagon with no sides to gauge the distance between the two parallel lines of railway track

gradient the measurement of the steepness of a slope

locomotive the steam or diesel-electric engine that hauls a train

ore rock containing metals

perforated having lots of holes

rack and pinion a system used to provide a locomotive with traction on a steep length of track. It consists of a length of metal rail (the rack) with spikes like teeth (pinions), running between the rails of the track. Locomotives designed to use the system have a cog wheel that rolls over the rack as the locomotive drives over it, giving the locomotive something to lock onto, preventing it from losing traction and sliding backwards.

railhead the end of the completed section of a railway line under construction

rail stacks stacks of rails stored at a railway construction site ready for laying

raw materials materials such as coal and iron ore involved in manufacturing industries

road trains long road tucks consisting of a number of connected sections

rolling stock locomotives, carriages and freight trucks

shunted pushed along the tracks

terrain the natural features of an area of land, such as mountains, rivers, and deserts

traction the grip wheels have on a surface that enables them to move

undercarriage the wheels and other mechanical parts that support a carriage, or locomotive

undulate rising and falling gently

viaduct a stone bridge supported by arches resting on pillars

Index

Abt, Roman 14
Alice Springs 8-13, 27
ballast quarries 12, 19
bogey exchange 5
cameleers 9, 31
camels 9, 16-18, 31
Central Australian Railway 8-13, 27
City Loop 20-25, 27
computer technology 22, 24, 26
Darwin 11-13, 27
earthworks 5, 18
freight trains 12, 31
gauges 4, 5, 7, 10, 13, 15, 16, 19, 26, 28, 31
geologist 16
Ghan, The 9, 10, 27
gradients 5-7, 14-16, 31
Kuranda Scenic Railway 28
Lithgow 6, 7, 27
locomotives 10, 11, 14, 17, 18, 26, 31
noise reduction 13, 24
Overland 28
pilot tunnels 22, 23
Port Augusta 8-10, 16-19, 27
Puffing Billy 29
Rails 4, 5, 11-14, 16, 19, 26, 30, 31
restoration 7, 14
safety 25, 26
sleeper factories 12
sleeper sling 9
sleepers 4, 6, 9, 11-13, 17-19, 24
stations 9, 18, 20-25
steam engines 7, 11
steam-driven cranes 9, 17, 19
surveying 7, 8, 16, 17, 31
Tilt Train 26, 27
tourism 7, 10, 14, 19, 28, 29
tracklayers 9, 13, 17, 18
Trans-Australian Railway 10,16-19, 27
tunnelling 4-7, 20-25, 28
underground railways 4, 20-25
West Coast Wilderness Railway 14, 15, 27
Whitton, John 6
working conditions 9, 15, 17
Zig-Zag Railway 6, 7, 27